Bedtime Stories for Ages 6-12

Bedtime Stories for Kids

Imogen Young

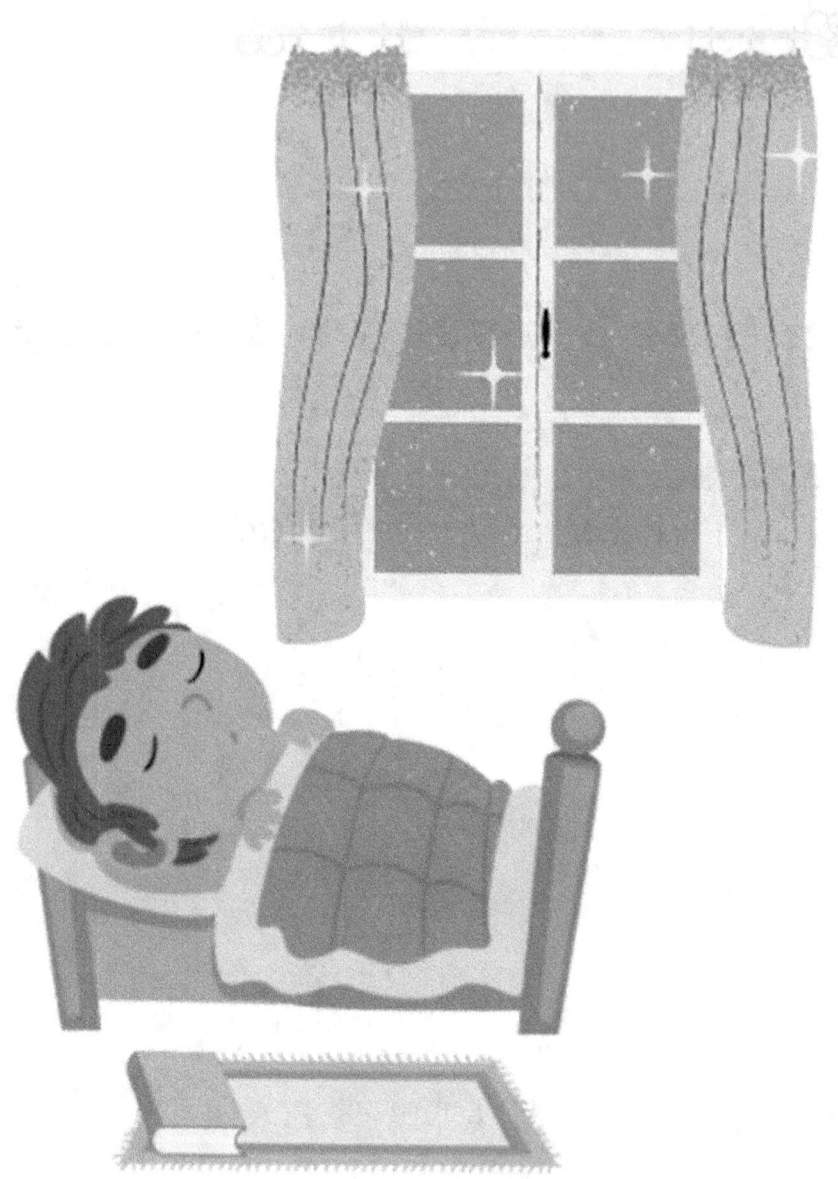

© Copyright 2021 - All rights reserved.

The content contained within this book may not be reproduced, duplicated or transmitted without direct written permission from the author or the publisher.
Under no circumstances will any blame or legal responsibility be held against the publisher, or author, for any damages, reparation, or monetary loss due to the information contained within this book. Either directly or indirectly.

Legal Notice:
This book is copyright protected. This book is only for personal use. You cannot amend, distribute, sell, use, quote or paraphrase any part, or the content within this book, without the consent of the author or publisher.

Disclaimer Notice:
Please note the information contained within this document is for educational and entertainment purposes only. All effort has been executed to present accurate, up to date, and reliable, complete information. No warranties of any kind are declared or implied. Readers acknowledge that the author is not engaging in the rendering of legal, financial, medical or professional advice. The content within this book has been derived from various sources. Please consult a licensed professional before attempting any techniques outlined in this book.

By reading this document, the reader agrees that under no circumstances is the author responsible for any losses, direct or indirect, which are incurred as a result of the use of information contained within this document, including, but not limited to, — errors, omissions, or inaccuracies.

Table of Contents

David 6
Grandpa Heinz 14
Travels 27
The Story of the Hare and the Tortoise 39
The princess 44
The Trials 58
The Grasshopper 98
The Dragonfly 104

David

David was very excited. It was his birthday and he got to do anything he wanted to do. Well, almost anything. His Mom didn't know anyone with a rocket ship that could take him to the moon. But the next best thing was the carousel in the park, and cotton-candy afterward! David knew exactly which horse he wanted to ride on too. The unicorn horse was his favorite. With the single long horn, it was the most special of all the

horses on the carousel.

His Mom once said that unicorns didn't even exist. But that was because last time they went to the carousel, a little girl was already on the unicorn and he had started crying. He was a lot bigger now and he didn't cry anymore. That was why his Mom had said they didn't exist. But David knew they did exist. Why else would there be one on the carousel? People wouldn't just make stuff up that was as important as unicorns. Or would they?

His Mom was waiting for him at the corner when he got off the bus. They were going right to the carousel. There was going to be a party later, and a cake, but it was riding the unicorn on the carousel he wanted most of all. When the music was playing and they were going around and around, and up and down, he was the happiest. David was sure that if only he believed hard enough, the unicorn would take off flying, and they would be flying over the city, and go wherever he wanted to go.

The trick was in believing hard enough, David told himself as they waited in line. He saw the unicorn coming by, then curving away. And then come back again, before again curving away. The music was playing and the lights were bright and spinning too. No one was on the unicorn. It would be his turn next. Except there was one kid and his Mom in front of them. He was kind of a goofy-looking kid and acting strange. David was sure he could get in front of him and make sure he'd get to the unicorn first.

But when the music had stopped and everyone got off, when the bell sounded, and it was their turn, the kid's mom picked him up and brought him right to the unicorn and put him on it! This was very unfair. David didn't have a chance of getting the unicorn. He turned to his Mom and said he didn't want to go, that someone was on the unicorn. David would wait to get on at the next bell.

"No David, we have to go now. There's no time and we have to get to the apartment. People are coming soon," she said to him. And his Mom almost dragged him onto the carousel. "Now pick another horse," she said. "I'll sit right here on the carriage bench."

David felt like crying. But he wasn't going to. He didn't cry anymore. But he wasn't going to pick another horse. "I'll just sit right here then, with you. Thanks a lot," he said. He looked at the boy on the unicorn. The boy's Mom was standing right next to him, and he was still acting goofy. It was like he couldn't even talk. That's how stupid the boy was. He couldn't even talk. "Look at that stupid boy," he said to his Mom, "he can't even talk. He's just drooling".

David's Mom looked at the boy, and it was clear to her the boy was severely disabled in some way. She'd seen the boy and his mother before in the park. His Mom was standing there to make sure he didn't fall off. The boy looked like he was very happy to be on the carousel. Unlike David, who could be a real brat at times. Surely, she then thought, David just didn't understand about the boy.

"David, that boy is disabled. You shouldn't say mean things about him. He's not stupid." David looked at the boy again as the bell sounded. "Why don't you go and say hi," she said. "Tell him it's your birthday. Invite him to your party. Go on now, I insist that you do it." When David's Mom used that word, insist, David knew it was best to do whatever she insisted. David went over to the boy and his Mom. The unicorn was starting to go up and down now.

"Hi," David said to them. The boy's Mom looked at him and said hello. "My Mom said to invite you to my birthday party today. What's your name?" he asked the boy on the unicorn. The boy was smiling and laughing as he went up and down. "His name is Charles, he doesn't talk much," the Mom said. "But he sure does love unicorns, don't you sweetheart?" The boy's Mom squeezed her son. She was holding onto him and Charles was laughing and nodded his head up and down as he went up and down.

"I love unicorns too," David said. "You know, if you believe in them – I mean believe in them – they'll take you flying. Did you know that?" "Well, of course, everybody knows that," the Mom said. "Especially Charles. He's flying right now. Would you like to fly too?" she asked David. David shook his head yes and said he would, very much. Charles' Mom then told Charles to hold on super tight to the pole, he reached down and picked David up and put him onto the unicorn behind Charles. "Okay, now hold on tight to Charles," she said, and David did.

David was on the unicorn and they were both going up and down, and around and around, the music was playing and the lights were bright. They were both smiling and happy. David then leaned up and whispered to Charles, who seemed delighted to have a riding partner, that he believed in unicorns. And that if Charles did too, they would both soon be flying over the city.

Afterward, Charles and his Mom sat with them while they ate cotton candy. Charles looked just about as happy as David felt while they both tore off chunks of the pink candy and giggled as it dissolved away sweetly in their mouths. Charles and his Mom even came by for cake later. It was the best birthday ever and David and Charles became very special friends.

Sharing what delights us makes it doubly delightful.

Grandpa Heinz

Tamara sits at the dining table with her grandparents - it's supper time. Grandpa Heinz once again tells the best stories. He used to be a sailor and experienced a lot. Granny Helene tells him over and over again he should not forget the food. But Grandpa Heinz is so in motion that he does not come to dinner. He tells of sea monsters, mermaids and waves as tall as houses. "You're going to spin your sailor's yarn again!" Says Granny Helene. "This is not a sailor's yarn Leni!" Says Opa Heinz. "Listen to me for the first time." "Oh," grins Grandma Helene. "You only give the little boy a fuss." After dinner, Grandpa Heinz proposes a walk on the beach. "Oh Heinz," says Granny Helene. "It's raining." But Grandpa Heinz is not deterred. "It almost stopped already. Plus, there's the right clothing for every weather, "he says, holding out the rain jacket to Tamara. "We'll be back in half an hour. Will you make us some hot tea? "He asks before Tamara and he walk out the door. And Granny Helene shakes her head and says what she always says: "You stubborn goat. Of course, I'll make tea for you. You should not get any snuff. " It is an uncomfortable weather. The sea is rough. But the rain has almost stopped. The rough sea reminds Grandpa Heinz of a stormy seafaring and he starts to talk. That's the beginning of a story that leaves Tamara quiet.

"I remember a seafaring trip that would hardly have survived your grandfather. It was a long time ago. I was still a young lad myself and did not go to sea much before long. The sea was even rougher than today and it stormed out of all the heavenly gates. The waves hit the cutter and the whole ship rocked back and forth. Some of the mariners were already afraid that the cutter would be full of water. So high hit the waves.

It was already dark and the rain whipped us in the face. In the dark we had lost sight and feared to walk on a sandbar keel. The best Kieker did not help you in the storm, you know? "Tamara looks questioningly at Opa Heinz:" Kieker? "" Yes, "says Opa Heinz. "This is a pair of binoculars. And before you ask, running a keel means the ship is stalling. "Tamara nods wide-eyed and with her mouth open. Then Opa Heinz continues: "Eventually I did not even believe that we would arrive home safely. We did not even know which direction we needed to go. The storm continued to grow and I no longer saw the hand in my eyes. Something suddenly shone in the water. At the light, I saw a little girl. Potz Blitz, I thought a stowaway had gone overboard and wanted to make my way to the bell. Then I saw the girl jump out of the water.

I could not believe my eyes. She jumped out of the water and into it again. Like a dolphin. But I tell you, that was not a dolphin. And it was not a little girl either. When I jumped out of the water, I recognized a huge fin. I'm sure that was a mermaid. Again and again she jumped in the air and turned, until I understood that we should follow her. She swam ahead and shone the safe way into the harbor. This little mermaid has saved our lives! But then I never saw her again. Grandma Helene never believed me that. But it is the truth." Tamara looks at Opa Heinz with an open mouth: "I believe you Grandpa. How did she look?" "Like a little girl. You could not see too much in the dark. I mean she had blond hair and a huge caudal fin.

It was really fast - faster than any boat I knew by then."

The rain has stopped and the sea has calmed down. A gentle breeze blows from the water and Tamara eagerly listens to every word that comes out of Grandpa Heinz's mouth.

What they do not know is that the little mermaid from Grandpa Heinz needs his help this time. And right now. Her name is Amelie. At that time, she told Grandpa Heinz the safe way to the harbor. Now she needs help herself. Only a few hours ago she had been playing with the fish at the bottom of the lake. Then the sea freshened up and Amelie realized that she had swum farther out than she wanted. For such a brave little mermaid that's not a problem you might think. But even for mermaids, the rough seas can be dangerous. Amelie swam toward the local cave vault, so she was not watching properly and a current seized her. She lost her footing and poked her head against a rock. Unconsciously, she was flushed to the beach and the tide set in. It is the same beach where Grandpa

Heinz and Tamara go for a walk. But the two are still too far away to help Amelie. However, a mermaid on land will not last long. Amelie wakes up and realizes that she is ashore. The ebb has pushed the sea far back. She wriggles like a fish on the dry land, but she does not get on well. She could have done a short distance. But the sea is much too far away due to the ebb. Discouraged, she gives up and bursts into tears. "Why does this happen to me? I've never done any harm. "She cries. "Oh darling, that has nothing to do with it." A voice suddenly says. Amelie swallows and wipes away her tears. But she sees nothing. "I'm up here," says the voice. Now Amelie sees a little fairy with beautiful wings flapping over her. "What are you?" Asks Amelie. "Well, what does it look like? I am a fairy godmother. To be more specific - your fairy godmother. But you do not have much to do as a fairy of a mermaid, "she smiles.

"Fairies do not exist!" Says Amelie. "There are only in the fairy tale." The fairy looks confused Amelie: "Oh dear. And that comes just from a mermaid? You know that mermaids are as mythical as fairies? "

Amelie shakes her head: "No, there are many of us in the sea. We're not mythical creatures. "The fairy touches his head:" Oh honey, what are they teaching you down there? "Then she makes two fists and holds them against her hips:" No matter, important now is that we get you back into the water. And fast! "

"But how are you going to help me? You are far too small to take me back to the sea. "Amelie says disappointed and close to tears again. "Sweetheart," says the fairy. "That has nothing to do with the size. Even little ones can help! "

Then the fairy thinks: "Hm, how was the spell for a stranded mermaid? You have to apologize. I'm out of practice. Most of the time you're in the water and I'm ashore. How was that again? " Then she swings her wand and murmurs a few words. The next moment the ground begins to fill with water under Amelie. The water becomes more and more, until Amelie is completely covered by water. The only problem is that the water is only around Amelie. She is swimming like a soap bubble now. The fairy exhales sadly, "It was not that," she says. Then she raises an eyebrow and says, "But we have gained time. Technically speaking, once you are back in the water. "Amelie nods and is happy to feel water again. But as much as the little fairy thinks, she does not come up with the spell. "It's getting pretty dark," she says. "I'll light up first." She waves her wand again and a small light floats next to her. "At least we can see something now." A few meters further down the beach, go to Grandpa Heinz and Tamara. When Tamara discovers the light, she excitedly points to the glowing something: "Da grandpa. The light you have been talking about. "Opa Heinz scratches his head:" No, that's just a lantern. There's still someone who can walk." "But it does not move at all." Tamara exclaims excitedly. She pulls Grandpa Heinz's hand. "Come on Grandpa. This is your mermaid! "

Grandpa Heinz wonders if Granny Helene was right after all. Maybe he should not have told the story. Maybe he just puts Tamara in the head with it?

Suddenly he sees his mermaid floating on a beach in a bubble of water. He stands stiff as a stick: "What, but what?" He says, staring at Amelie. Tamara is quite outraged: "Da grandpa, you see? I told you. Is that the mermaid who saved you? "And Amelie recognizes Grandpa Heinz again. "You've gotten older," she says.

"But I recognize you!" Before the fairy could hear that, she's already flapping on Grandpa Heinz and boxing him with her little arms against his nose: "Stop!" She exclaims. "You will not touch Amelie, otherwise you will get to do it with me!" Grandpa Heinz carefully reaches for the fairy: "It's all right. I will do nothing to her. We know each other. "The fairy looks surprised Amelie over:" Is that true? "Amelie nods.

Grandpa Heinz comes closer to Amelie: "So your name is Amelie?" He asks. Then he points to Tamara. "This is my granddaughter Tamara." Amelie greets Tamara, who has now stopped babbling and standing with her mouth open. "You are beautiful!" Says Tamara and Amelie thanks.

Grandpa Heinz extends his hand to the water and says: "I could never thank you. You have saved my life! "At that moment, the fairy hits him on the hand:" Stay away from my water. "Then she waves her forefinger:" Touching the figure with the paws is forbidden. And now you go. We have work to do! "

The fairy flutters to Amelie and tries hard to push the bubble of water. But she does not move. Amelie is too heavy. "I'll help you," says Opa Heinz and just wants to push with, as the fairy cries out: "NO! I said do not touch! "Grandpa Heinz stops jerking.

"If you touch the bubble of water, it will burst or worse!" The little fairy is just catching her breath as she sees little Tamara push the bubble of water out of the corner of her eye. "But how is that possible?" Asks the fairy. Amelie nods to the fairy, "It's alright. Tamara is my soulmate. As I had felt with Heinz at that time, I feel it now with her. And I will eventually feel it with their children. "And Tamara pushes the little mermaid back into the sea. As Amelie is back in the sea, she jumps happily in the waves around. Then she shows up and waves to Tamara: "Thank you dear Tamara. We will meet again! But now I have to go back, "she says, turning around and disappearing in the waves. When Tamara turns around, the fairy is gone as well. Grandpa Heinz stands further back on the beach and beckons Tamara to himself. "Come on, little one, we have to go back, too. Granny Helene is already waiting for us with the tea. " When they arrive at home Tamara tells how a waterfall. The story gushes out of her: "And then I pushed the mermaid back into the sea. She waved me once more and then disappeared. Even the fairy was gone then. "Granny Helene strokes her cheek:" Well, you have experienced a real adventure. But now the tea is drunk and then it goes into the trap. " After Grandma Helene Tamara has gone to bed, she looks at Grandpa Heinz and smiles: "What did you do with her? She talked all the time until she fell asleep. The sailor's yarn that she spins does not fit any more. "Grandpa Heinz only smiles back and nods:" There's so much out there. And stories want to be told. Let her dream! " Then grandma Helene and grandpa Heinz go to bed. And Grandpa Heinz is happy that he now has someone who believes in him and shares his stories with him. Even if it will remain a secret between the two. Tamara and he know there's a little mermaid out there called Amelie, who will always watch over them at sea.

Travels

There are many ways to travel where you want to go. Trains, cars, trucks, buses, and boats are all great modes of transportation. Another great mode of transportation is airplanes. Airplanes fly high in the sky above everything, helping people get to their special destination with ease. For many people, airplanes are a mode of transportation that they use regularly to help them get where they are going. For example, politicians and musicians use airplanes to get to important meetings or concerts that they are hosting worldwide! For Noah, airplanes were brand new. He had never been on an airplane before, and he had no idea what to expect. Noah's grandpa wanted to take him on a special trip to the other side of the country to visit a special museum, but he could only do that if they were going to fly. Trying to drive that far would take a long time, and trains were more expensive to ride on and often took longer to get to their destinations. With an airplane, though, Noah and his grandpa would be across the country in just a couple of hours. Noah thought it was very cool that a plane could travel so fast and that they would get there almost no time. As they were getting ready for their trip, Noah began to get nervous. He was excited to ride in an airplane with his grandpa, but the idea of going somewhere new and then being so high scared Noah. He did not know what it would be like to go through the airport or ride in an airplane. Noah worried that maybe he would get scared or feel uncomfortable while he and his grandpa rode the airplane.

While he packed his bags and got ready for his trip, Noah's dad tried to comfort him so that Noah would feel more comfortable with the trip he was going to take with his grandpa.

Noah's dad told Noah that taking the airplane would be easy. He told him that they would check in their luggage, and the airport attendees would make sure their luggage got on their airplane. They would then be checked through security to make sure they were not carrying anything that might be unsafe to carry on an airplane. Next, they would wait in a big sitting area for their airplane to be called; then, they would get on the airplane. Once they were on, they would fasten their seatbelts and listen to the pilot tell them what to expect. Then, they could watch TV on the airplane while a flight attendant brought them snacks and drinks. Noah's dad told him that by the time they were done eating and drinking, the flight would almost be done, and they would get off. They would get their luggage from the luggage trolley and make their way to their car so that they could go to the museum! Noah did not think it sounded too hard to ride an airplane, but he was still worried about all of these new experiences. That night, he had a difficult time sleeping as he wondered what it was going to be like and how he would do during his first time flying. Even though Noah was scared, he was still very excited to go on this special adventure with his grandpa.

The next morning, it was time for Noah's ride on an airplane. His grandpa came to his house and put his bags in the car while Noah said goodbye to his parents. By now, he was feeling both very scared and very excited about this special trip he was taking with his grandpa. After he was done saying goodbye to his parents, Noah and his grandpa got in the car and headed toward the airport. Noah told his grandpa that he was scared and excited at the same time, and Noah's grandpa said he understood. Then, he told Noah the same things his dad had told him about what to expect and how easy it would be to take it. Noah started to feel more comfortable and tried to relax as they made their way to the airport.

When they got to the airport, Noah's grandpa parked their car in a special parking lot, and then they paid for a special ticket that let Noah's grandpa leave his car there until they got home. This way, they would have a car to drive home in when they got back from their trip! Once the fare was paid, they walked into the airport and started getting ready to get on the plane. First, they went to the luggage area and gave their bags to the luggage attendants. As they did, the luggage attendants placed tags on their bags that let the airport know which flight those bags needed to be on. They then signed papers to confirm that their bags had been checked and kept a piece of paper for confirmation. Once they checked their bags in, they made their way to the security checkpoint. This part felt scary for

Noah, as there were many sounds, machines, and people all over the place. Everyone had formed lines toward the checkpoint so that the security guards could make sure that everyone was safe and ready to travel.

This part took a while as it took time for each person to be checked in through the checkpoint for them to get to the waiting room. Noah watched as each person took off their jackets, shoes, and any jewelry that they might be wearing to put them in a bucket with their bags. The bucket would then go down a conveyer belt through a metal detector, and then the people would walk through a separate metal detector. On the other side, the security guard would make sure everything looked proper and safe, and then they would let the passenger through to the waiting area. Finally, it was Noah and his grandpa's turn to go through the security pass. Each of them took off their shoes and jackets, and Noah's grandpa took off his wristwatch. Then, they put their carryon bags on the conveyer belt. One by one, they walked through the metal detector, and their bags went through the metal detector, too.

On the other side, the security guard checked to make sure that everything was okay, and then they were given their stuff back. They set their jackets and shoes back on, and also Noah's grandpa put the wristwatch of his back on. Then, they grabbed their carryon bags and headed to the waiting area. The waiting area was just a big lounge filled with chairs and a few airport stores. One store was a convenience store with snacks and drinks, and the other was a book store. There was also a restaurant in case people wanted to eat before they took their flight to wherever they were going. Noah looked around at all of the people who were waiting, eating, and shopping for books. He was surprised by how many people were in the waiting area and wondered how many of them would be taking the flight with him and his grandpa. Noah and his grandpa found a seat and waited for the attendant to call their number so that they could board their airplane. When she did, they got up and went to the lineup, showed the attendant their boarding pass, and then started to board. Boarding the airplane was unusual: they walked down a long hallway and ended up on the plane at the end. Noah thought it was cool that they could attach this hallway to the airplane and get on the airplane this way. Once they were on the airplane, Noah and his grandpa found their seats and sat down. It took a while for everyone to board the airplane.

Noah and his grandpa watched as families, men, women, and business folks all piled on. Each found their seats, put their bags away, and then sat down and waited as the rest of the passengers boarded. Finally, after what seemed like forever, everyone was on board, and the airplane was ready to take off. They started takeoff with a message from the pilot.

The pilot talked to them about the flying conditions, and what to expect in terms of turbulence. Then, he talked to them about safety measures and what to do if there was a problem with the airplane.

This made Noah worry, but his grandpa assured him that everything would be fine. When the pilot was done talking, the big TV at the front of the plane turned on, and Noah was offered headphones from the flight attendant. He and his grandpa each accepted a pair and turned them on to listen to the movie that was being played while they flew.

Then, they took off.

Take off was a cool experience for Noah. It started with them driving down the runway, but soon they were going so fast that the plane took off into the air. They took a sharp turn upward, and within moments they were flying through the clouds. Soon, they were above the clouds and flying straight to the other side of the country. Noah seemed out the window to see the tops of the clouds and, once the clouds parted, the towns which fell below them. Most of the cities were too far away for Noah to see anything other than the texture of the ground, but he still thought it was very cool. While they flew, Noah looked out the window, watched the TV, ate the snacks, and drank the attendant's drinks. Then, just like his dad said, by the time he was done, the plane was almost getting ready to land. As they got closer to their destination, the pilot came on the radio again and told all passengers about their landing. He let them know that it was time to put their seatbelts back on and that they would be landing very soon. He told them what time they would be landing at, what to expect, and what to do during the landing process. Soon after, they landed on the runway. It was a bit of a bumpy experience, but it was over quickly. Once they landed, Noah and his grandpa got off the airplane by going down a similar long hallway like they had when they boarded the airplane. Then, they went and collected their bags and went outside to catch the taxi to their hotel.

The

rest of the trip was very exciting for Noah. They stayed in a hotel, went to the museum, and enjoyed delicious dinners and breakfasts from the restaurants near the hotel. By the time their trip was done, Noah was sad to leave all of the fun behind but was excited for another ride on an airplane. Noah thought airplanes were so cool, and he could not wait to go on another trip on an airplane again really soon. He even asked his grandpa if they could go back to the museum again soon! Noah's grandpa just laughed and said sure.

The Story of the Hare and the Tortoise

A long, long time ago, there was a forest where a group of animals used to live.

- You know what? I am the fastest all around - Said an arrogant rabbit standing in front of the crowd. - Nobody can beat me in a race –

- Yes! It is true! I have seen him running and I bet he can beat anyone in this forest. – said an elephant, convincingly.

Suddenly, they heard somebody laughing in the crowd:

- Why are you laughing? Do you think you can run faster than I can? – said the rabbit, quite annoyed.

- While I do not disagree with you, Mr. Hare, I would like to say that I am afraid to compete. – said a tortoise, bravely.

- Oh… Is that so? Well, why don't we race? Let's see who wins. – replied the rabbit.

On a fine sunny day, all the animals in the forest gathered for the race. Everybody was sure that the hare was going to win:

- May the best man win! – said the tortoise, wisely, while he looked at the rabbit.

- And that is me. - said the hare, proudly. - Now, let's go my friend. I will beat you in a second. -

The hare ran so fast that everything on his path seemed to spin. On the other hand, the tortoise ran too, but so slowly that even snails went by quickly. Everyone was laughing at the tortoise. Suddenly the hare stopped and looked behind him.

- Oh, my, I cannot believe my eyes. That tortoise is going to take ages to reach this point. So, I think I will stop here and give it a rest. By the time he reaches me, I will have enough rest to cover him in the blink of a second. – said the hare with arrogance.

In the meantime, the tortoise slowly and steadily reached the point where the hare had fallen asleep. He very quietly tiptoed past the hare. The hare was sleeping so deeply that he didn't even hear him.

Suddenly, the hare woke up when the crowd roared and cheered for the tortoise:

- Go, tortoise, go! Go tortoise! – shouted the crowd.

- Oh, my, how is this even possible? I slept for so long that the tortoise is about to win this race. – said the rabbit.

The rabbit started running and ran as fast as he could, but to his great dismay, the tortoise finished the race before he did.

The princess

There once was a lovely young woman who lived in the sea. She was born in the sea and knew only of its properties and its abundance. Her father was the King of the Realm, and guarded her aggressively, as he loved her more than life itself.

Her name was Ari, and she was a mermaid. Ari often swam close to the land and popped up to the surface to watch the men on the beach and in the neighboring town. She was lonely and had begun to feel restless with her life under the sea. She wanted so very badly to walk like the land women she saw on the beach and find a landman who would love her and want to take care of her always.

One day, she went to see her Fathers Sorcerer and told him about her dreams and desires. The Sorcerer was aware that the King had bid her never to speak of the land species and that to ever leave the water's safety was never going to be allowed. He knew that, and she knew that, but he came up with a plan, and on the following week, he called Ari to his chamber.

Ari was intrigued by the Sorcerers plan and became very excited. She had been spending more time watching the people on the beach than ever, and she knew that she would never be happy until she was able to go forth unto the world of the walking and find her mate. She listened carefully, as the wicked Sorcerer outlined his plan and agreed to all of its terms. The plan was kept a secret from the King, as she knew her Father would lock her in her chamber for an eternity if he found out. She had the Sorcerer make up a potion that she would drink and become a landlady, but there was a catch. She would only be able to stay a landlady for one week before she would again turn into a mermaid.

On the day she had set aside to swim to the water's edge and then drink the potion, she made herself look as pretty as she possibly could, and then left the King's domain. As she swam nearer to the water's edge, she became nervous. "What if the potion doesn't do the job, and also I get stuck over the land forever? What if the potion doesn't work, and I start to be ugly and old and stuck on the area forever?" she thought. Then she stated to herself, "You are being ridiculous. The King's Sorcerer may be the finest, and he'd never earn such a ridiculous mistake."

Ari swam on her back for some time going over what it would be like to be human, walk on two legs, and do human things like fall in love. "Fall in love," she whispered to herself; "Fall in love?" yes, that is what she wanted, so she would go ahead and drink the potion. With that, she pulled out the vial the Sorcerer had given her and drank the entire thing down. Then, she began to feel very strange but in a very good way. Her vision blurred for the moment, and she felt light-headed and drifty. Then, everything changed, and she felt as though she had been sleeping for all of her life and not had woken up. She felt happy, alive, and excited all at the same time.

Ari looked around at the beach again; only this time, the beach looked like she would have to go if she wanted to go home, and the deep ocean looked like a place to go if she wanted to explore. "The potion has worked beyond all my expectations!" she thought to herself. "And now, for the ultimate test of its power," she thought as she looked down at her tail. The tail was nowhere to be seen and in its place were two long, slender, and beautiful legs. "This will do nicely!" she exclaimed aloud, "Very nicely."

She immediately began swimming for the shore, and for the first time in all of her years, she put her feet down and felt the sandy bottom, the sand between her toes, and the movement of legs and feet. Something she had been dreaming about for so very long. Then another first. Ari was now in the shallow waters near the ocean's very edge, where it meets the sandy beach. She looked at the beach now only a matter of feet from her and watched as the water lapped up and down on the seashore. It was a beautiful sight to her as she could never have come this close to land before when she had a tail instead of these two wonderful legs, as she could have easily become stranded and then discovered by the humans. Everyone had warned all the children in the realm that if the humans ever caught them, they would poke and prod them and put them in cages and treat them like a freak. Nobody should need to endure such therapy, the king had instructed them.

But these days, she could easily walk out of the bath and up the beach and speak with whomever she pleased. For the first time in her life, she was standing, and she enjoyed this brand new feeling. This's great! she referred to as away aloud. What's great? a male's voice nearby asked. Ari was shocked and stunned. She had never heard a real man's voice spoken over the air of the planet. She turned to see an old man wearing a pair of ugly bathing trunks standing not 20 feet from her. "Oh, hello," she said. "I was just planning a party for my husband," she lied, "And I thought of a great way to surprise him." She continued. "Oh, so it's a surprise party, eh?" the man muttered. "What? Oh Uh... yes, that's right. A surprise party for my husband." And then she turned and walked for the very first time. She walked like a real woman that she indeed was on that day. She walked with confidence. She walked with character and charisma.

"But where was she walking to?" she began to wonder. "Oh no," she thought. "I did not think this through very well. Now, what do I do?" she asked herself.

She saw a small building with a palm leaf roof and noticed many people sitting on high chairs and leaning on a long platform. They were all facing the same way and laughing and talking, and most were men. "Right." She said to herself. "I'll go there and join them."

As she approached the shack, most of the men suddenly became all in a bother and began shuffling around to look at her. One of them let out a strange whistling sound that came from his mouth. "Well, hello there, sweetheart!" the closest one said. "Hey, there, honey. There's an open seat here by me. And it's open forever for you, baby!" another one claimed. She noticed all of the men were asking for her company except for one. He was way down at the other end of the platform and was very handsome. She headed towards him and was in luck. There was an open seat on the very end of the platform on the other side of the man. She walked right up to it across the sandy beach and climbed up into that high chair.

There was another man whom she had not noticed on the other side of the platform, and he had on a funny outfit. It was not a bathing suit like all the men on her side had, but had bright red and white colors on it and quite ugly. She tensed when she saw the strange man behind the platform walking straight towards her. "What'll it be, miss?" the man asked her. She froze. She had no idea what he was asking her or why he was even talking to her.

She stared at him for a moment and then said, "I don't know," which was the truth. He thought she meant she didn't know what she wanted and said, "Okay, miss, I'll check back with you in a few minutes." And went back to fiddling with his glasses and bottles. The gentleman whom she had sat beside turned to look at her, and she found herself hypnotized by his bright blue eyes, dark curly hair, and smile.

Then he spoke. "I'm John Blake," he said, and then he waited. She knew she was supposed to say something, but she didn't know what. Her name! That was it; he wanted to meet her. Of course! "I'm Ari," she said finally and then turned to face forward again. He did not stop looking at her, and in fact, he held out his hand in a way she had never seen. His thumb was facing up, and his little finger down, and his hand was stiff like a knife. She turned and made her hand into the same gesture. He looked down at both of them, holding their hands out in a ridiculous fashion, quickly took her hand with his, bobbed their hands up and down a few times, and then let go of it. "How strange," she thought.

A bit more time passed, after which the handsome Mr. Blake turned towards her once more and said, I was thinking whether you'd love to join me for a stroll on the beach? Ari's face lit up because this was one thing she did understand, and she liked the male very much. I'd like to, she answered with a smile. The 2 slid off the barstools of theirs and walked down towards the water then down the beach. They walked and talked for over one hour and became very good friends. Next, she recognized he was a little anxious, and she guessed she was too. This was wonderful. She'd walked out of the water and into the life of a tall, handsome stranger.

Suddenly, out of the blue, John asked her, May I buy you dinner tonight? Before she knew what, she was doing, she agreed, but there was a problem. The Sorcerer had forgotten to provide her with the complete story. She needed cash and clothes and who knew what else to function on the dry land world. Realizing that she was in a bit of a jam, she quickly made up a story about how she had been on vacation with some girlfriends and had become separated from them.

That day, they were scheduled to board a bus somewhere and get to the airport, and now all she had were the clothes on her back and nowhere to stay. He bought the story and took care of everything. They went to the clothing store and purchased some fine items for her and then went to dinner. After dinner, she went home with him, and he let her stay on his couch, but before long, they fell in love, and he wanted her to stay forever. Of course, she couldn't do that but continued to make up stories about why.

Eventually, they became very happy together, and he began asking questions she had no answers for. This made her very uncomfortable, so she decided to tell him the truth. "You're a Mermaid?" he said with an astonished look on his face. Ari was amazed at how well he took this incredible information and was even more in love with him. How would they do it? What could they do to make it work now that he knew her complete truth? Then John had an idea. He told her that he was a scuba diver, and he asked her what she thought of him coming out into the water for some visits, and then she comes up on land like she was then on other visits.

That plan seemed like the only one that could work. "I'll buy a sailboat," he said. "And I can pick you up, and you can be yourself and be with me on the boat. We can sail around and have lunch, and well, what do you think?" he asked. She was overjoyed at the idea of having truth between them and agreed.

In the months that followed, John and Ari spend every spare moment together. Sometimes swimming together and playing in the ocean and sometimes sailing which as it happened, she loved. She had never been on a real sailboat, and John was a great sailor. Then, one day, she went to the Sorcerer and asked him if he could change her permanently into a land walker. He was very worried about what the king would think but then figured out how to make it, so she had control over her body. She could be herself in the water and share precious moments with her father, and she could be the land girl and be with her man whenever she liked.

Soon, John asked her to marry him, and after learning what marriage meant, she was very happy to marry him. As time passed, Ari spent most of her time with John, but just enough time with her father, so he did not suspect anything or get angry because she was spending so much time away. That was how our story went, and anyone who read it was charmed by the little girl who grew up as a Mermaid and did meet her prince charming.

In the end, she had three wonderful children, and to her relief, they all had human legs and were perfect babies. She was sad she couldn't tell the Father of her but pleased that she'd achieved her dreams beyond what she'd ever thought possible.

Never let go of your dreams!

The End

The Trials

There is a place I know that's far away but easy to find. You can't find this place on any map on earth. But you can visit any time that you want. It is a magical place where dinosaurs walk and talk just like people. Dinosaurs have their own lives, just like we do. They can think and feel, make friends and laugh and play. I can show you how to get to this place. All you have to do is listen and follow my instructions.

The first thing I want you to do is to breathe in and slowly. A deep breath in, and then a deep breath out. There, that wasn't so hard, was it? I don't think so either. Now I want you to think very hard about the past. Not yesterday, not the day before that. Not last week or the week before that. I want you to think way back. A long, long time ago.

Imagine how it was before you were born. Imagine what was going on in the world. You weren't around to see it, but the world always existed without you. It's a little hard to think about, isn't it? Well, that's okay. Just try your best. And if you can't think about anything, then just continue to listen to what I say. There is no right or wrong way to do this.

Do you ever think about what happened a long time ago, before we had cities and cars? Do you ever imagine how life was for the people that lived before technology? Let's go a little further. A long time ago, people had to ride horses instead of driving in cars. This was a long, long time ago, even before your parents were born.

But we can still imagine it, can't we? It's very easy. Instead of getting in a car to drive to the store, people had to walk there. Or if it was far, they had to take a horse. I think you get the idea. But we can go farther than this still. We can imagine how things were like before people appeared.

I know this is difficult but just imagine. A long time ago, there weren't any people. Millions and millions of years ago. Do you know how long a million is? It's a long time. But we can still think about it, can't we?

Millions of years ago, some dinosaurs walked the earth. Nobody knows where they came from or where they went, but the dinosaurs existed. They were big, scary and full of scales. If you think about it, most dinosaurs were just really big lizards.

I want you to imagine this right now. Imagine going back in a time machine to when the dinosaurs still existed. How do you think life was then? Were there any roads back then? What about houses? Could you still walk down to the store to buy some candy? Probably not. But what you could do was walk down the jungle and find Stegosaurus with all of its pointy spikes. Or maybe you would see a pterodactyl flying through the air. Maybe you would see a volcano erupting.

Did you know that back then, you could find bugs the size of cars? Well, it's true. A long time ago, they existed. Today bugs are very small, and boy, am I glad. We can step on them with our shoes. But if we lived a million years ago, it would be us getting stepped on by them! Can you imagine something like that? Imagine a big bug that could squash you.

It's a little scary, but this is the world of imagination. And you can imagine just about anything. Go ahead and try it. Imagine a world very different from ours—a world where you can find dinosaurs and other creatures roaming the earth.

I want to welcome you now to a place I know. It is called Dino Land, and here you can find all sorts of friendly dinosaurs there. You might even say that the dinosaurs that live there are very much like us. They have feelings just like us, and they also have dreams. They also like to make friends and have a good time.

Does that sound like fun? Well, all you need to enter Dino Land is a big imagination. I want you to think about a world very different from ours. A place is full of colorful dinosaurs, big tall trees and green grass. Now, if you think you are ready, you can follow me there.

This is my trusty time machine, and all I have to do is press a few buttons, a knob there, a lever here and a viola! Our destination of Dino Land is only a few minutes away. While we wait, I want to warn you. Dino Land can be a scary place. But I promise you that the dinosaurs that live there are all very friendly. You will see.

The time machine makes beeping noises, and then you hear a big crash. I think we have finally arrived! Now let me just open up the hatch here, and we can get out of this thing. There we go! I think you should go first. Consider it my gift to you. Just crawl out of that little hole there, and on the other side, you should see Dino Land. Ready? Okay, go!

What do you see? Do you see the tall trees as big as buildings? Or what about the tall grass that covers the ground? I think we landed right outside of the jungle. If you look, you can see a bunch of trees behind us. The jungle is dark and scary, so maybe we shouldn't go that way.

So far, we haven't seen any dinosaurs, have we? But we can still hear the sounds of the birds coming out of the jungle. And the rustling of the leaves as they move in the wind. If we listen carefully, we might hear the sound of a dinosaur walking. Remember that they are really heavy and they make the ground shake when they walk. Tremble, tremble, shake shake.

A little bit up ahead, you spot something truly strange. Something that you didn't expect to see in a million years. But since this is your imagination, anything is okay. What you saw was a big wooden fence that seemed to go on forever. In the middle of the fence is a big wooden gate, and above that, there is a sign, and it reads "Welcome to Triceratops Ranch."

And this is where our story begins. On the plains of Dino Land, Triceratops Ranch is where all sorts of Triceratops like to hang out. It's a place where they can play with friends and have a good laugh. Here they can eat all the grass that they want and live out their lives.

Triceratops ranch is a very peaceful place. The breeze is easy here, and there aren't so many trees. Should we enter Triceratops Ranch and see what it is all about? I think we should. Triceratops is a type of dinosaur with four legs. It has a big tail, and on its head, there are three big horns. They have a big head that looks like a shield. Their head bones have a type of armor that is tough. It's good for headbutting things. The Triceratops doesn't feel a thing.

Do you hear that noise? I hear laughter and yells, like the sound of children playing. Let's go check it out. A little further into Triceratops Ranch and we see our first dinosaur. Well, group of dinosaurs, I should say. There's one, two, three, five baby triceratops playing a game of tag. It looks like a lot of fun!

Let's have a listen and hear what they have to say.

"Tag! You're it!" Said Cecilia. She was a light brown girl triceratops. "No, you are it!" Said another named Johnny. A boy triceratops

"Tag no tag backs!" Said Tabby. She was another girl triceratops with small horns.

The youngsters seemed to be having a lot of fun. And though they were just babies, they still made the ground shake a little every time they passed by. Oh, don't worry. They can't see you. We are using the power of imagination, remember? We are just here to see where the story takes us.

"Trish, come and play with us!" Said Tabby to another triceratops who was far away.

Trish was a cute yellow girl triceratops, but she looked worried. Something was wrong, and her friends didn't know what was wrong.

"Trish, what's wrong?" Asked Johnny. "Is everything okay?" Trish shook her head. She looked very sad.

"I think I'm in trouble," said Trish. "The Elder said he wanted to talk to me. But I didn't do anything wrong."

The Elder was the head dinosaur on Triceratops Ranch. You could think of him as the principal of the school. He was the wisest and the oldest dinosaur that lived on the ranch. Whenever something went wrong, you went to see the Elder. Trish didn't know why the Elder wanted to talk to her, but she was very worried about it.

Trish's friends tried to cheer her up. Trish was a very shy dinosaur who didn't like to talk much. She also followed the rules, and never got in trouble. So you can imagine why Trish was sad. She was no trouble maker. Why did the Elder want to talk to her?

"It's okay, Trish," said Cecilia. "He probably just wants to ask you something"

"Did he say you were in trouble?" Asked Johnny.

"Maybe he wants you to help with the pumpkin festival" said Tabby.

That was right! The pumpkin festival was coming up, and every year the Triceratops make decorations and set up a little festival full of pumpkins.

Trish was looking forward to it this year.

"But why me?" She asked. "Of all the dinosaurs that live on the ranch, why would he ask me?"

"Well, there's only one way to find out,' said Johnny. "You have to go see him"

Trish squealed with fear. Her little legs were so shaky that she almost fell over.

"Don't worry," said Tabby. "We will go with you"

And so, the group of young Triceratops made their way to the grass fields where the older Triceratops were having lunch. It wasn't hard to spot the Elder. He was the oldest and the biggest Triceratops that there were. He wore lots of jewels that said he was the boss. Each horn had many necklaces made out of rocks and beads.

The Elder liked to eat alone, so when they found him, he was all by himself. Trish tried to hide behind the backs of her friends, but the Elder quickly spotted her. She wanted to run, but it was too late.

"Ah, Trish!" Said the Elder in a booming voice. "Come here, please"

Trish and her friends walked up to the Elder at the same time, together. It made Trish feel a little less scared.

"Hello Johnny, Cecilia, Tabby" Said the Elder. "I hope you are all having a good day today"

"We sure are!" was Tabby. "We were playing tag in the field, and we even saw a butterfly!"

"Did you want to see Trish?" John Asked the Elder.

Trish could feel her cheeks getting hot as she turned red with embarrassment. She did not want John to bring it up. And now Trish was put on the spot by her friend. She knew he was only trying to help, but it was no use.

Have you ever been in a situation where your friend embarrassed you? Trish is very shy, and she blushes a lot. This happens when your face gets warm and turns red like a tomato. There is nothing to be ashamed about blushing. But for a shy dinosaur-like Trish, it felt like the end of the world.

"I see you all came to me at once!" Said the Elder. "And yes, I did want to see Trish. That is why I called her over. But I didn't call any of you!"

Trish felt even more embarrassed now. Her friends gave each other looks and nodded.

"I would like to speak with Trish privately, please," said the Elder. "You all can continue playing once we are done talking. Come now, Trish, let's go for a walk."

The other dinosaurs stood behind and watched as Trish walked next to the Elder. She was even more embarrassed than before, but the Elder didn't seem to notice it. Her friends trying to help, but there was nothing more that they could do.

"Sorry, Trish," said the Elder. "But I have something very special to talk to you about today."

Trish had no idea what he meant. But it didn't sound like he was mad at all. Instead, the Elder seemed to be in a good mood. Maybe she wasn't in trouble.

"You see, Trish, every year a dinosaur on Triceratops ranch is chosen to make a journey."

"A journey?" Asked Trish. "What do you mean"

"We call them the trials of the Triceratops. They are a series of tasks that every Triceratops needs to complete. If you do, you will be welcomed to the herd"

"I don't understand" Said Trish.

"If you pass the trials, which I think that you will, you will be officially a member of our tribe. You will be given new responsibilities on the ranch"

"But what if I don't complete them?" Asked Trish feeling a little scared now. She never heard of the trials, but she did remember that her big brother had to leave on a journey a long time ago. When he returned, her brother was stronger, and his horns got bigger.

"You can always try another year again," said the Elder. "But I and the rest of the tribe have chosen you because we think you can complete them. You must retrieve the three magical eggs. They are scattered in areas away from the ranch. One in the Gola swamp, one in the Shifty Sands, and the last one is on Three Point Mountain"

The Elder gave her a special pouch to keep the eggs inside. Once they were safe, the eggs would be protected by the pouch. If she returned to the ranch with all three eggs, then she would pass the trials of the Triceratops.

Trish had never left Triceratops Ranch all by herself. The eggs were scattered far away, and she would have to go on a journey away from home. She didn't want to do it. She knew that she couldn't do it.

"I can't," she said to the Elder. "I just can't"

"Yes, you can." said the Elder. "You can do this, Trish. You will see. Go now, go on your quest. And don't come back until you have found the eggs"

"But!" The Elder gave her a scary look, and she knew that she had to do it. There was no other way.

When Trish told her friends, they were all amazed that she was picked for the trials. And they all convinced her to go.

"It will make you stronger!" Said John showing off his muscles.

"Show them you have what it takes, Trish," Said Cecilia was patting her on the back.

"We will be cheering you on!" Said Tabby.

They all promised to meet up at the pumpkin festival when she returned.

The first place that Trish decided to go to was the Gola swamp. It was the closest egg to the ranch. The only problem was that the Gola swamp was a stinky and scary place. There were even rumors that it was haunted. Trish was terrified out of her mind. But something told her she had to go. It was her duty to get the eggs back to the Elder.

Trish walked to the gates of Triceratops Ranch, and without looking back, she crossed them. Now she was out in the wild, all by herself and ready to start her journey. She felt free like never before. She would stay on the other side of the fence and not know what went on outside it. But not today. Today she would see the outside world on a journey away from home can be a scary thing. And in Dino Land, it was no different. Can you think about a time that you had to do something alone like Trish? Was it scary? And how did you overcome that fear?

Sometimes all it takes is a little bravery.

Trish walked and walked through unfamiliar lands. She walked until she couldn't see Triceratops Ranch anymore, and she was completely alone. The grass started to grow taller, the trees got bigger, and she heard strange sounds from the forest.

She knew she was getting close to the swamp because the ground started to feel mushy, and her feet started to feel heavy. The swamp also started to smell bad. A triceratops is heavy. Even baby triceratops can weigh as much as a car. What if she got stuck in the mud? Nobody would be able to find her there. What would happen to her?

She was really scared, but she knew that the more scared you get, the worse it feels. She just had to find the egg, but it was nowhere to be found. She didn't even know where to look. All that she could think about was what if she saw a ghost.

"Oooooooh" Came a voice from the swamp. "Ooooooh!"

"Who's there!" Said Trish as loud as she could. But there was no answer.

 Only the same "Oooooh" noise from before. And it was getting louder and louder.

"Ooooooh! Ooooohh!"

The swamp was haunted! Trish got so scared that she ran away as fast as she could. The ground was still muddy, causing Trish to trip and fall. She thought something was chasing her, and she ran and ran until she couldn't hear the scary sound anymore.

"Trish! Trish! What happened?"

She turned around, and she saw John and the other's following her. "What are you doing here?" she asked.

"We couldn't let you go alone, Trish!" Said Cecilia. "When we heard you went to the swamp all alone, we had to follow you!"

It was just like before when her friends took her to see the Elder. It was like they were babysitting her. She felt bad. Not because she was scared, but because her friends thought that she needed help. Friends are like that sometimes. And they just wanted to help.

"I don't need your help!" Said Trish. "Go back to the ranch and leave me alone!"

Trish knew that she had to do the task on her own. If she didn't, it wouldn't count, and the Elder would know.

Her friends tried to stay and support her, but they saw all upset Trish got and ran away. Trish felt like she was going to cry. But she had to keep going.

"There is no such thing as ghosts," she said to herself as she walked through the swamp.

"There is no such thing as ghosts!"

Then she heard the same noise from before. "Ooooooooh! Ooooooooh!"

"There is no such thing as ghosts. There is no such thing as ghosts"

Trish closed her eyes and walked deeper and deeper into the swamp. She could barely move anymore when her face hit something hard. Trish opened her eyes and in front of her was a glowing, green egg. She did it! She found the first egg!

She put the egg in the pouch, and she heard the voice of the Elder speaking to her.

"Congratulations, Trish, you have completed the first task. The egg would only show up if you entered the swamp alone, and that is exactly what you did! This magical egg will give you the power of courage as you continue your journey"

With the egg in her pouch, Trish no longer felt scared. She walked through the swamp-like it was nothing. She knew that the noise she was hearing was probably just the wind passing through the trees. That had to be it. After a while, she learned that there was nothing scary about the swamp at all.

She decided to go to sleep and try to find the second egg in the morning. Shifty sands were very different from the swamp. Instead of trees and grass, there were rocks and sand everywhere. The ground there was very flat. Trish wasn't used to it at all. The wind was very strong, and it got in her eyes, making it harder to see.

"I just have to find the egg." Said Trish. "Then I can go home"

But doing so was going to be easier said than done. Every time the wind picked up, it caused a huge dust storm, and Trish couldn't see anything until it passed. Sand got everywhere on her skin and face, almost burying her.

Ever since she found the first egg, Trish stopped being scared. Like the Elder said, it was a magical egg that gave her the power of courage.

Now she was just annoyed. The sand kept burying everything. She tried looking for the egg, and the sand would come in and cover everything up again. Finding the egg was going to be impossible. Tiny pieces of dirt and rocks bounced off her tough dinosaur skin.

Only a triceratops could finish this task. If you or I were in that sandstorm, we couldn't do it because the tiny rocks would cause too much damage. Even when the storm got worse, Trish held her ground. All she could hear was the wind rushing in her ear, and all that she could see was the color of sand. On the floor and in the sky, it was everywhere.

She didn't really know what she was looking for. Her only thought was to try digging in the sand, and if she was lucky, the egg would be there. Last time she had to stumble on the egg on accident. Maybe that is what she needed now. Just a happy little accident that would show her the way to the egg.

Unfortunately, Triceratops isn't the best diggers. They have stumpy legs and are missing the sharp claws that would allow them to dig through the sand.

Instead, Trish had to rely on her purse strength to move the sand around. And it wasn't going so well for her.

"I've had enough!" She said, spitting out a mouthful of dirt. "I'm going to try again tomorrow and see if the wind has come down a bit"

And that is exactly what she did. The Elder only said that she had to collect the three eggs. He didn't say when she had to collect them or if there was a time limit on her return to Triceratops Ranch. So Trish decided it would be easier to rest for now and to try the next day again.

She got up extra early because she thought the wind would be less strong in the morning. But when she got there, there was almost no difference. Shifty Sands remained just as windy as before. Trish didn't care. Once, she tried her best to find the egg by digging into the ground. And once again, the wind kicked sand in her eyes and mouth. A thin layer of dirt covered her entire body.

Trish looked like a walking pile of sand by the time she gave up once again. She shook her entire body to try to get the sand out, but a bunch of it stuck to her skin. She had to take a bath to get it all out.

"Maybe tomorrow the wind goes down," Trish said to herself as she walked away from Shifty Sands in defeat.

"Surely it won't be this windy two days in a row," She thought.

But in the morning, she would find out that she was dead wrong. The wind continued, and Trish struggled with all her might to find the egg buried in the sand. And once again, she couldn't find it and ended up giving up after the sand was up to her knees. There had to be a better way.

The next day it was the same story. And the day after that. And even the next day. Trish was finally beginning to lose hope. There was no way she could see the egg in the middle of the sandstorms. Did the Elder play a dirty trick on her? Or did he expect that she would be able to see through the sand? She was a triceratops, not an armadillo!

Then, on the sixth day, Trish saw that the winds had finally stopped. The sand was calm, and the rest of the desert looked at peace. The only problem now was that Trish noticed for the first time just how big the desert was. How was she expected to find the egg now when the sand went on for miles?

Trish walked into the desert as far as she could before the wind started to pick up again. This time the sandstorm was so bad that she had to close her eyes. And it was there, in the middle of the sandstorm, that Trish felt something smooth and hard in between her feet. Whatever it was, she put it into her pouch and instantly, she heard the voice of the Elder speak to her.

"Well done, Trish! Well done! You have found the second magical egg. This egg is the egg of perseverance and hard work. Because you never gave up on your quest and continued to try day after day, this egg now belongs to you. This egg will allow you to continue on your quest without getting tired so fast."

She couldn't believe her eyes and ears. Finally, after days on the quest, she had found the egg. She was just about to give up and return to the ranch when she mysteriously found the egg on in the sand. And now that was safely put away in her pouch. She felt full of energy.

That day Trish walked for many miles, and not once did she feel tired. The magical egg was doing its thing. Her feet didn't hurt as much, and she didn't stop to nap. Her next destination was Three Point Mountain. And there, she would find the last egg and bring it back home.

Three-Point Mountain was a big hill covered with rocks and boulders. They called it three points because there were two smaller mountains next to it.

Trish knew that she would have to climb up the highest one, all the way to the top. And that only at the top would she find the last egg. She just knew it would be there.

But getting to the top would be no easy task. The rocky terrain was difficult to walk on, and it was very steep. One false move and Trish could be sent rolling down the hill. Huge boulders moved around often, and you might see one coming straight for your face.

If that wasn't bad enough, Three-Point mountain was an active volcano that erupted several times a day. Just how on earth was Trish going to make it up there? She already had two magical eggs in her pouch. One made her unafraid of things, and the other made her tireless. Those were going to be a big help on the way up. If she didn't have those eggs, there was no way she could climb up.

The ultimate challenge was just about to start. Trish took a big breath and took her first step up.

"I can do this," she said to herself. "I can do this. And I will do this!"

Trish was motivated to find that last egg. She had come too far to go back home empty-handed. And after she found the egg, she would officially be part of the triceratops tribe. The Elder and the others would see just how strong and tough she was.

At first, the climb was easy. Little bits of rock crunched under her heavy feet as she went up. But then moving up was getting harder and harder. The mountain side was getting steeper, and Trish had to work twice as hard to cover half the distance.

And the higher she went, the harder it becomes to breathe. Trish knew only one thing about climbing up mountains, and that was to never, ever look down. If you looked down, then you started to panic. And if you panicked, then you might fall off, and that would hurt a lot.

Up ahead, Trish came to a flat area. Suddenly the mountain stopped being so hard to climb. But she saw something strange in the distance. There was a bridge in the middle of the mountain, and the only way she could get to the other side was to cross it. There was no other way up.

Trish could tell that she was high up already because the trees around her looked like tiny little heads of broccoli. She even thought that she could see Triceratops Ranch from where she was.

"Don't look down, Trish. You can do this. Just don't look down," she said to herself. She put one leg on the bridge, and it made a nasty creaking noise. She didn't like that at all. But then she put down a second leg, and a third and then a fourth. The bridge was able to hold her weight after all.

"Don't look down. Trish. Don't look down"

But she did look down. It's a little hard for a triceratops to look straight all the time once you think about it. They aren't very tall, and they have to see their feet and look out for their horns. But she did. She did look down. And it was terrifying. Under the bridge were a big river and sharp rocks. Trish did not know how to swim.

"This is bad. This is bad. This is bad," she kept repeating to herself. She was still saying it when she felt her foot touch solid ground. Amazingly, she made it through the bridge without issue. But that was only the start of her problems because as soon as she got off the bridge, she heard the volcano erupting.

Hot steamy lakes of lava were coming down from the mountain top. Trish would have to play the ultimate game of the floor is lava to get to the top.

And this time, it would be for real. She could have turned around right about then, crossed the bridge again and went home. But she was so close to the top that she just couldn't do that.

The mountain rose higher and higher. The flows of lava went in every direction, sending up smoke in the air every time they collided with a tree.

 Trish heard a loud rumbling, and she thought it was an earthquake. But she looked up and saw that it was a large boulder that was coming straight for her.

Being brave is a good thing, but a dinosaur still has to know when it is time to run. And this was a time for her to run, hard and as fast as she could. The boulder made its way down the mountain, and it somehow got past the rocks and the lava. Trish moved as quickly as a triceratops could, and the boulder missed her.

She was almost to the top of the mountain. The lava was everywhere now. The heat made her sweat, and she could see steam rising from the molten rocks.

She needed to find the egg fast, or she was going to be dino toast. But Trish wasn't scared, even when her feet started to feel hot from the lava. All she needed to do was to find that egg.

Then, at last, she saw it. The egg was a shiny red color, and it was lying inside a nest. The only problem was that there was lava surrounding it. The only way that Trish could reach it was if she made a big jump and landed right next to it.

"It's now or never," said Trish backing up a little to get speed. If there is one thing that a triceratops is good at, it's charging. And she was about to make the hardest charge that she ever did in her life. She got ready to make the charge by stomping the ground with her paw. Little bits of dust went in the air as she did it.

Trish charged with all her might and yelled "I can do it" as hard as she could.

She looked down after she made the jump, and she saw the lava just below her belly. But it was too far away to touch her. She could feel the heat underneath her stomach, but she still soared through the air and landed right next to the egg.

She did it!

As soon as she touched the egg, she heard the voice of the Elder talking to her once again.

"Congratulations, Trish, you have completed all three trials. You are now officially part of the triceratops tribe. You have shown your courage, your hard work, and you never gave up"

Trish placed the egg carefully inside the pouch and the two other eggs, and she heard a loud screeching noise in the sky above her. It was a big scary flying dinosaur coming straight for her! There was too much lava, and she couldn't move. The flying dinosaur lifted her into the air and carried Trish away.

"Let go of me!" Trish yelled. She had to make it back to Triceratops Ranch and return the eggs. No matter what.

"It's okay," said the dinosaur that grabbed her. "I was told to bring you home. You have finished your trials."

Trish felt a great relief. She was so happy that she started to cry. She didn't have to climb down the mountain again. She didn't have to cross the bridge or tiptoe through the lava. And she didn't have to cross Shifty Sands all over again. She was going home.

The other dinosaur dropped her off just in front of the Triceratops Ranch gate. She landed softly on the ground, and she was really glad to be back on the floor instead of the air. All around her, the pumpkin festival was starting. The other Triceratops had put up decorations, and there were pumpkins everywhere. The biggest pumpkins that she had ever seen.

Her friends saw her and gave her a big hug. She was finally home. And she was stronger and tougher than ever. It was just like the Elder said. He knew that she could do it. All she had to do was to believe in herself.

"Welcome back, Trish!" Said the loud booming voice of the Elder. "We all knew that you would come back. Just in time for the festival too."

"But the eggs!" Said Trish looking through the pouch. "They are gone!" "They have returned to their places," said the Elder. "For the next triceratops to make the same journey as you."

Trish spends the rest of the day playing with her friends and eating all the pumpkins that she could. She deserved it. And it was all thanks to Trish being able to believe in herself.

So the next time that you find yourself scared and unsure that you can do something, be like Trish. Know that anything is possible through courage and a little hard work. And so, that is the end of this story. I hope that you enjoyed traveling to Dino Land just as much as I did. But for now, I say good night. And until we meet again, go with peace.

The Grasshopper

A grasshopper was newly arrived at a forest and didn't know anyone who lived there. He didn't know the first thing about the old Owl who lived in a large oak tree, a tree close to where he just then was. The grasshopper didn't know that nobody who lived in the forest liked the Owl. He was new to that forest.

Stories were often told about how mean this cranky old Owl was. The Owl liked to sleep during the day, and if anyone bothered him, the Owl would throw down stones or sticks down upon them. The old Owl was known to have even done far worse.

The grasshopper knew nothing of the old Owl. And as grasshoppers do, while he was standing by the tree looking around, he started singing. It was nothing at all for a grasshopper to sing. Grasshoppers sing about anything. They sing about the trees or the wind, they sing about the sky or the grass. It doesn't matter. And this grasshopper sang very loudly.

Suddenly, a stick came falling from the tree, and the grasshopper looked up. He saw the Owl peering out from its nest, looking quite angry. "Be quiet, I tell you, be quiet," the old Owl yelled. "I can't sleep with all the noise you're making down there". The grasshopper quieted down .

But not for long. Soon after, he started singing again. Everyone knows grasshoppers sing as easy as they breathe. This time a stone came flying down and almost hit him. He looked up and saw the old Owl, now very, very angry. "I won't ask you again. Be quiet!" the Owl said. The grasshopper stopped. But after only a little while, he started singing again.

The cranky old Owl was furious. But he knew the grasshopper wouldn't stop, no matter how many stones were thrown. The Owl would have to try another way to get some peace. The Owl came down from the tree, and said, "Well hello, grasshopper. Aren't you a wonderful singer? Perhaps you'd like to come up and have some tea with me, so I could hear you sing more closely."

It seemed like a fine to the grasshopper. He would enjoy having tea and making a new friend in the forest where he knew no one. However, what the grasshopper didn't know was that the Owl enjoyed eating grasshoppers and would happily have him for lunch. When they got up to the Owl's in the tree, he went in.

"What a beautiful home you have," said the grasshopper. "Please, make yourself comfortable," replied the crafty old Owl. The Owl made tea and they both sat at chairs, not far from each other, but not too close either. The Owl poured the tea and asked the grasshopper to sing a song and the grasshopper did. Afterward, the Owl exclaimed, "What a lovely song. But come a bit closer, therefore i can hear the following song better".

The grasshopper moved a little closer and sang another a song. When he was finished, the Owl said, "Well, quite lovely, quite a lovely song. But do come a little closer. I'm old and hard of hearing. I'd like to hear you better".

The grasshopper moved even closer to the Owl and sang another song. The Owl replied, "You sing more beautifully than anyone in the forest. If only my hearing were better. Come just a little closer".

The grasshopper moved so close he was almost sitting in the Owl's lap. But this time, before the grasshopper could start to sing, the Owl snatched him with his beak and gobbled him up!

"That will teach that grasshopper to keep an old owl from sleeping with silly songs", Owl said.

The Dragonfly

There was a dragonfly who lived on a small lake. The dragonfly loved to fly over the reeds along the banks of the lake. All-day long he would fly back and forth, skimming over the water, along its edges with reeds. He liked very much to hover along, just inches over the water's surface, then pull up and be just inches over the reeds, looking down and the wonder of the lake just barely underneath him.

Some ducks were nesting in the reeds. They had a nest full of eggs, and the eggs would soon hatch. The mother and father duck would enjoy taking turns sitting on the nest. How peaceful and perfect the world was, the ducks would be thinking. Until suddenly, they'd hear the droning of the dragonfly come close, and the ducks would duck their heads. They were afraid the droning dragonfly would run into them. They would soon be busy enough raising their ducklings. They needed rest to gather their strength for that.

The ducks came up with a plan to rid themselves of the pesky dragonfly. The next time it came along, they yelled for it to stop for a second. The dragonfly did stop. He asked the ducks what the matter was. The ducks told the dragonfly about a beautiful lake that wasn't far away, just on the other side of the woods that stretch alongside the banks. The ducks said they'd heard it was so beautiful, that they were thinking about going there with their ducklings, as soon as they hatched.

"Well, thank you", said the Dragonfly. "Maybe I'll go look at this lake myself, then come back and tell you about it".

"Oh, could you, Mr. Dragonfly", they said. "How very nice of you. Thank you very much". And the Dragonfly left right away into the woods, the other side of which was the lake. Or so the ducks had said.

In a little while, the eggs hatched and the little ducklings soon came to swim in a neat line behind their mother and father. The dragonfly had gone on further and further into the woods and never found the lake. But he did find a stream, and he buzzed often alongside its banks.

One person's pleasure can be another's annoyance.

www.ingramcontent.com/pod-product-compliance
Lightning Source LLC
Chambersburg PA
CBHW070936080526
44589CB00013B/1526